FART JOKES FOR SMELLY KIDS

by **Dawko & Ditz**

Illustrations by

This book belongs to_____

who farted_____ times today.

Dawko; 1969 -
Ditz; 1964 -
Hackett, Dave; 1970 -

Fart Jokes for Smelly Kids

ISBN 978-0-9944471-0-4

Typesetting by Dawko. Typeset in Adobe Garamond Pro 16pt.

Manufactured in Australia
Printed in Australia by Ligare Pty Ltd, Riverwood – ligare.com.au
First printing October 2015

Also by Dawko & Ditz

The Bum Book

Also by Cartoon Dave

Gross Cartooning
The Summer of Kicks (Young adult novel)
Time for Bed, Daddy (picture book)
Cartoon Dave's NO-RULES Cartooning
Cartoon Dave's Fab Face Freakout
M.A.D Cartooning (Monsters. Aliens. Dinosaurs)
Hands On Cartooning   *Unstoppable Brainspin*
UFO – Unavoidable Family Outing   *Sumo Granny Smackdown*
UFO in the USA   *Norman Enormous*
UFO Afloat   *Hamilton's Handstand*

Not in any way at all

∧LEGAL DISCLAIMER

By opening this book you declare that you are, indeed, a Smelly Kid™ and that you take delight in making all kinds of sounds and smells with your bum.

Any farts which result from excessive laughter while reading this book remain the property of the farter, except where the stench enters the nostrils of any other person (hereafter to be known as "the fartee").

LET THE JOKES BEGIN!

How do bums get all their ideas?

They put on their stinking caps!

How many bums does it take

to change a light bulb?

Just a phew!

No, really, how many bums does

it take to change a light bulb?

Fart too many to count!

What do stinky koalas eat?

Bum leaves!

What instrument does a bum play?

Fluteus maximus.

FLUTEUS MAXIMUS

What has two cheeks and something

in the middle that smells?

Your face!

Where do bums go on holidays?

The Great Barrier Reek.

What's brown and smells?

A dog's nose.

What's another name for a stinky mutt?

A poo-ch!

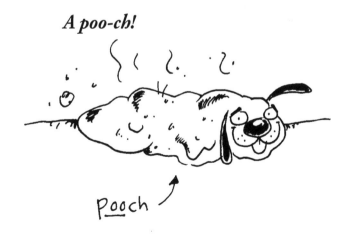

Pooch

What has a long body and wears smelly undies?

A dacks-hund.

Which is the stinkiest of all dogs?

A poo-dle.

What does a bum wear to rob a bank?

A gas mask.

What's brown and smells like poo?

Poo!

What else is brown and smells like poo?

More poo!

Where does a teddy bear do its poo?

In the toy-let.

Which volcano is the smelliest?

Mt Crack-atoa.

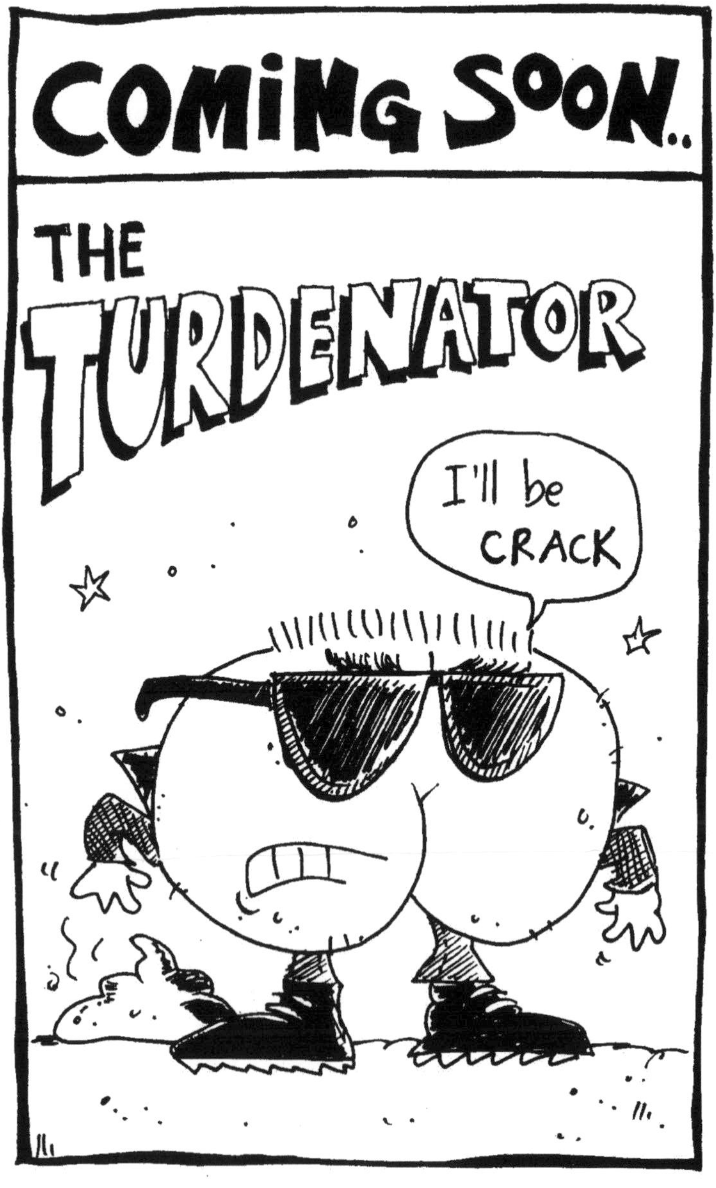
COMING SOON..
THE TURDENATOR
I'll be CRACK

A DAY AT THE POO ZOO

What looks like a llama and stinks?

An al-crack-a.

What looks like a donkey and has a huge crack?

An ass!

What kind of turd has thick skin and huge jaws?

A hippopootamus.

HIPPOPOOTAMUS

Which antelope does the worst farts?

A gaz-smell.

Which is the smelliest cow?

A bum steer.

What has big horns, eats grass and smells terrible?

A cari-poo.

What kind of poo has a hard shell?

A turd-tle.

TURD-TLE

What kind of poo has lots of legs and eats leaves?

A scat-erpillar.

Which insect is the prettiest AND the smelliest?

A butt-erfly!

Which insect is the loudest AND the stinkiest?

A crack-et.

Which marsupial leaves marks in its undies?

An e-skid-na.

Which insect farts all the time?

A bum-ble bee.

What is the smelliest

Australian marsupial?

A Kangapoo.

Which animal is the fastest AND the smelliest?

A cheek-tah.

What do you get if you cross

a rooster with a bum?

Cock a Doodle Poo!

(COCK-A-DOODLE-POO)

What enormous reptile

really smells bad?

A crack-odile.

What do you call a monotreme with diarrhoea?

A splatypus.

What is the largest and smelliest creature on earth?

A poo whale!

VAMPIRE BUTT

What's big and white
and stinks all over?

A poo-lar bear.

Which of the big cats stinks the most?

A poo-ma.

What's smelly and
has beautiful feathers?

A turd of paradise.

What do you call a
lobster with diarrhoea?

A spray-fish.

What fish farts the most?

A hali-butt.

●━━━━━━━━━━━━━●

WHAT HAS A SPINE, BUT NO BUM AT THE END?
A BOOK!

BUSTING FOR A POO

by
Anita Dunny

21

BOOKS

CAN I GET TO THE TOILET IN TIME?
by May Knott

OOPS!
by Will Knott

WELL, WHAT HAPPENED?
by Deedee May Kitt

WHAT A MESS! by E. Mist

WHO'S CLEANING THAT UP? by Y. Mee

HOW DOES THAT SMELL?
by
Terry Bull

FARTING MADE EASY
by
Ben Dover

What did the bum die from?

A bad case of poo-monia.

What do you call an evil bum's helpers?

Stenchmen.

Where do poos get held prisoner?

In the dung-geon!

What did Godzilla do after he ate Tokyo?

A city dump!

Which Olympic event is the best

for constipated athletes?

The triple dump.

What's round, yellow and stinky?

A custard fart!

Why did the toilet go red?

It was flushed.

How long does
a fartnight last?

Two cheeks.

What is the smelliest

nursery rhyme?

Plop Goes the Weasel.

What do you hear when Prometheus does a poo?

Splash of the Titans.

What does Thor wear on his bottom?

Thunderpants!

What's stinky and robs you out at sea?

A poo-rate.

Not-so-Jolly Roger

Who was the stinkiest of

all the poo-rates?

Craptain Crackbeard.

What does a poo-rate

say to his poo crew?

Arr, me farties!

Which are Australia's stinkiest cities?

Skidney!

Smellbourne!

Poocastle!

Ballarsplat!

Bumdaberg!

Bowelral!

WHAT HAS TWO HALVES & A BIG CREASE DOWN THE MIDDLE?
A BOOK!

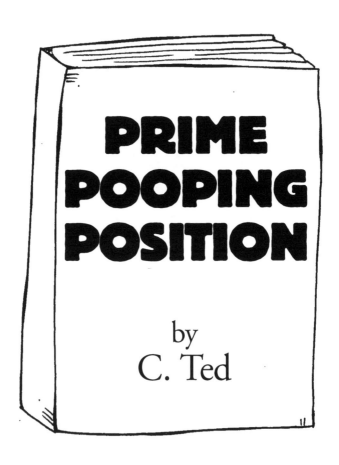

TOO MANY BOILED EGGS

by
Con Stipated

ROTTEN CURRY

by
Di Arrea

BIGFOOT'S BUM

by
Harry Cheeks

DOG POO ON THE GROUND

by
Lee Vitt

"I SMELL POO — Oda Russ"

Why did the witch call a plumber?

Bubble, bubble, toilet trouble.

How does blood get to your bum?

Through your farteries.

What's round and stinky?

A hula poop.

What is a bum's favourite magazine?

Poo Weekly.

What's the smelliest vegetable?

Fartichoke.

When do bums sleep in?

On cheek-ends.

How does a bum interrupt you?

It butts in!

How do bums greet each other?

They say "smello".

What do you call a poo that's

really eager to come out?

Dung-ho!

What do you yell to scare away a poo?

"Scat"!

What do you call a baby poo?

A dumpling.

What do you call a baby bum?

A crack-ling.

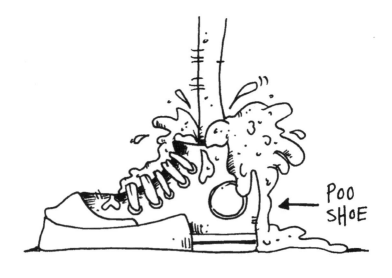

POO SHOE

I'M NOT POOING, I'M DEEP IN THOUGHT

If a baby kangaroo can't stop farting, is it a

blowy joey?

If you do a fart and it makes a hooting

sound, do you think you might have an

owl bowel?

If you do a fart and it makes a lot of short clucking

sounds, do you think you might have a

fowl bowel?

If a large group of cattle all get diarrhoea,

does that make them a

turd herd?

What TV shows do bums love to watch?

Sit-coms.

What is a bottom's favourite flavour jam?

Raspberry.

What is brown and on the end of a stick?

A lollipoop.

How do you know when a clown has farted?

It smells funny.

What does a pachyderm wear on its bum?

Ele-pants!

What do you call a poo that's nearly extinct?

An endangered faeces.

What do you call it when an
entire species farts itself to death?

Ex-stink-tion!

What do bums do for self-defence?

Fart-ial arts.

What kind of fart-ial arts do most bums do?

Kung-poo, and poo-jitsu!

SUMO BUM

Doctor, doctor!

My brother thinks

he's a bum!

It sounds like

he's cracked up.

Doctor, doctor!

No matter how hard I

try, I can't break wind!

I think you need

a fart transplant.

COUNT CRACKULA

Doctor, doctor!

My bum keeps giving

me advice!

Is that a wise crack?

What does a doctor

use to make your

bum numb?

Anus-thetic.

I'M STILL NOT POOING, I'M DEEP IN THOUGHT

If everyone at your birthday breaks wind, is it a

farty party?

If a scientist launches an air missile, is she a

farty smarty?

If two bums have a deep and meaningful

personal conversation, is it called a

fart-to-fart?

If you step on a sharp

weed and it farts, is it a

windy bindi?

If everyone in a daycare

centre farts is it a

windy kindy?

If you do a fart and it's really

deep and long, is it called a

bowel growl?

If you do a fart and it's really

high and piercing, is called a

bowel howl?

Which bicycle really smells?

A penny-farting.

What does a poo see at his school reunion?

Lots of familiar faeces.

What kind of book is 'Fart Jokes for Smelly Kids'?

A Best Smeller.

What do you call a dumb bum?

A nincom-poop.

Where does a bum like to swim?

In a Poo-l.

What do you call a bum

that operates on your brain?

A poo-rosurgeon.

What do you call a

bum with feathers?

A crack down!

If you lose your bum, where

can you buy another?

At the re-tail shop.

What do you get if you

cross a bum with a laptop?

A com-poo-ter.

Where do bums go to learn?

A poo-niversity.

Why do bottoms like school?

They learn the alpha-butt.

Why do bums fart?

They don't know the words.

What has a head but no bum?

A coin.

What did the shark say to the boat?

I can see your bottom.

Why does a school band stink?

It has a wind section.

What is the best day to go to the toilet?

Poosday.

What is the second best day?

Turdsday.

Why are clouds so smelly?

They fluff all day long.

What do you call a witty bum?

Cheeky!

Why should you never listen

when a bum tells jokes?

Because they all stink!

What's twice as smelly as a bum?

Two bums.

Where do bottoms keep all their photographs?

In an al-bum.

What do bums eat for breakfast?

Bubble and squeak.

What do you say when your sister's son farts?

Ne-phew.

What do you find at the bottom of the forest?

Underplants.

What do you call undies

when they've gone missing?

Underwhere?

What does the Easter Bunny wear on her bottom?

Hot Cross Bun-dies!

Which days are best to change your underpants?

Mundies!

What does Dawko wear under his

jeans when he's writing these jokes?

Pun-dies.

WHAT LOOKS NOTHING LIKE A BUM BUT WE WISH IT DID FOR THE PURPOSE OF MAKING UP A SUPER-CLEVER HEADING FOR THIS PARTICULAR SECTION?

A BOOK!

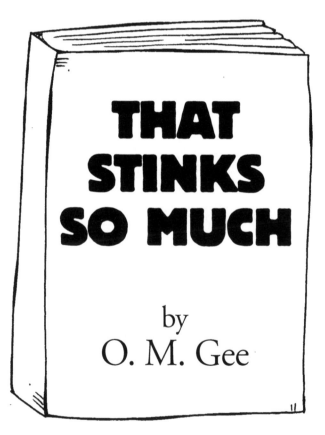

THAT STINKS SO MUCH

by
O. M. Gee

SHARK FARTS

by
Indi Ocean

WHERE'S EVERYONE GONE?

by
Ivor Smellie-Butt

HOW MUCH POO CAN YOU DO?

by
Laurie Lode

MORE THAN ONE TOILET CAN TAKE

by
Phil Dupp

AFTER CURRY FARTS

by
Lee Thall

RAN OUT OF TOILET PAPER

by
Hans Dirty

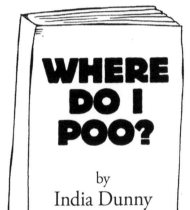

WHERE DO I POO?

by
India Dunny

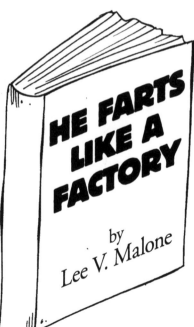

HE FARTS LIKE A FACTORY

by
Lee V. Malone

BLOATED BELLY
by
Lotta Gas

COULDN'T GET A POO OUT
by
M. T. Bowl

HAVEN'T POOPED FOR WEEKS
by
Dustin McCrack

66

I LIKE BIG BUTTS

Anna Kennett-Lye

I'M NOT STINKING, JUST DEEP THINKING!

If a ballerina takes a dump, is it called a

tutu poo-poo?

If a train driver drops a
stinky load, is it called a
choo-choo poo-poo?

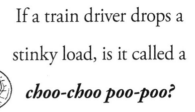

If you do a poo and it's
really short, is it a

stumpy dumpy?

If you drop a load while you're
doing a somersault, is that a

loop-de-poop?

If you sit on a computer and fix it, do you have

geek's cheeks?

If a police officer takes a
dump, is it called

cop's plops?

If your dung is too soft, is it a

droopy poopy?

If you poo while you're
climbing a ladder, is it

rung dung?

If a poo gets annoyed, is it a

grumpy dumpy?

POOPY LONGSTOCKING

If your underpants smell so bad

you knock people out, are they

stun-dies?

If Santa's undies fall down, is he

Saint Knickerless?

If Attila wore knickers, would they be

Hundies?

If you can't work out which pair of
briefs to wear, does that mean you're

undies-cided?

If your briefs always know what
you mean, does that mean they're

undies-standing?

If you vomit and it runs down into
your briefs, does that make them

chunderpants?

What's a bum's favourite snack?

Chocolate crack-les.

When two bums argue...

do they butt heads?

Who made all the bum's

dreams come true?

His airy godmother.

What does a Reverend Mother

wear under her clothes?

Nun-dies!

How does one bum talk

to another bum far away?

Smellular phone.

What kind of music do

bums like to listen to?

Poop music.

Where does a bum

wash its dishes?

In the kitchen stink!

I'M NOT DEFECATING,
(pooing)
I'M CONTEMPLATING!
(thinking really hard!)

If you poo first thing in the morning, is it called an

AM BM?

If you poo in the afternoon, is it called a

PM BM?

If you hear a poo on the radio, is it called an

AM/FM BM?

**BM?
What the?**

*BM stands for "bowel movement",
which is a polite way to say "POO!"*

If you run out of toilet paper and
use terry cloth, does that make it a
bowel towel?

If a computer expert forgets to
flush, is his toilet filled with
nerd's turds?

If a piece of poo gets attacked
by bees, is it called
stung dung?

Dude- you totally STING-K!!

If a rock band drops a load
while they perform, are they a
poop group?

If your bottom keeps
tripping over, is it a
stumble bum?

If your bottom played
guitar, would it be a
strum bum?

If your crack runs straight up
and down, does that mean it's a
plumb bum?

Who is the stinkiest dancer?

A smell-erina.

What do you call steamroller farts?

Flatulence.

What do you get if you eat dynamite?

Explosive diarrhoea!

What do you call a bum that paints?

A fartist.

Which musical instrument is a bum's favourite?

Cracksophone.

Which is their second favourite?

Poo-phonium.

What church instrument is powered by farts?

A ripe organ.

What is a bum's favourite day?

Farter's Day.

What is a bum's favourite punctuation mark?

The colon!

Which vegetable is always farting?

Aspara-gas.

What is a bum's favourite dessert?

Raspberry fart.

Where does a bum buy groceries?

A poo-permarket.

Why did the bum cross the freeway?

To show everyone it wasn't a chicken.

What does a baby bum need in a car?

A pooster seat.

Last week my bum turned ten.

You know what we sang him?

Crappy birthday!

What do you call a bottom that always comes back?

A bum-erang.

What's pink, hairy and makes a terrible smell?

A piglet!

What does a bum do at a gym?

Crack-sercise.

What does that bum wear

while it's working out?

A crack suit.

Why is a bum always calm

after it farts?

Because it's feeling smell-ow.

What is a bum's favourite game to play?

Hide and squeak.

Which kind of duck has

the stinkiest bum?

A smellard.

What sound does it make?

Crack, crack.

What goes traf, traf, traf?

A bum breathing in.

Where do bums live?

An afartment block.

What game does a bum

play with its baby?

Peek a poo.

Which cartoonist is the smelliest in the world?

Dave Crackett!

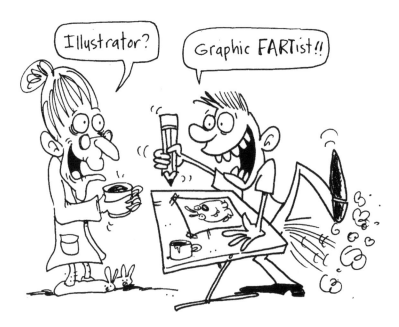

What do you get when you cross

a flying saucer with a bum?

An Unidentified Farting Object!

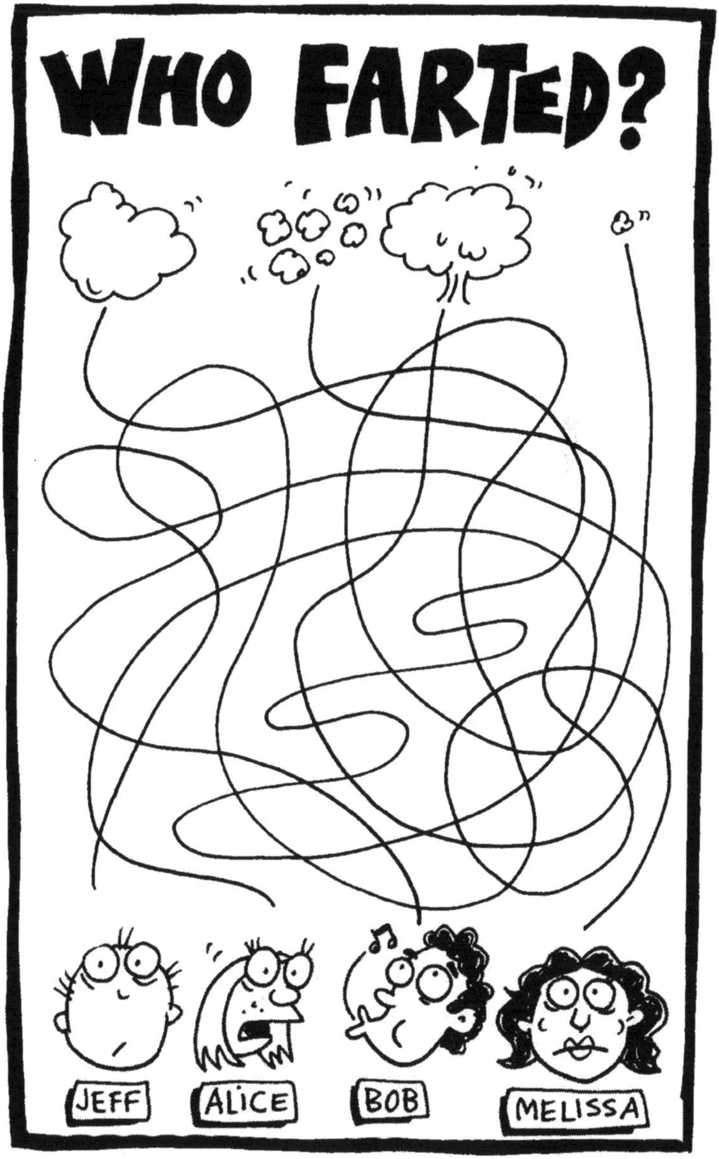
WHO FARTED?
JEFF
ALICE
BOB
MELISSA

BUMMER, DUDE!
WE'VE REACHED THE...
END!

BUT KEEP YOUR HAIR ON!

WE'LL BRING YOU MORE
BUM-BASED HILARITY
BEFORE YOU KNOW IT!

About The Authors

Dawko

A fellow named Dawko, I hear

Was known for his loud stinky rear

Make sure that you're not

Up too close to his bot

Or you just might not hear for a year

You can contact
Dawko via email at:
dawko@y7mail.com

Ditz

I know of a lady called Ditz

Who farts every time that she sits

At parties when there's

Games of musical chairs

It sounds like a flatulent blitz!

Cartoon Dave

There once was a fellow called Dave

Who didn't know how to behave

The noise from his bum

Scared his dad and his mum

So they sent him to live in a cave

You can contact Dave via email at: **dave@cartoondave.com**
or check out his website: **www.cartoondave.com**

ALSO BY US!

With facts made fun and a healthy dose
of imagination, this book will appeal
to parents, teachers and kids of all ages.
The Bum Book really will put "bums on seats"!

Available from **www.thebumbook.com.au**
and also from Amazon!